THE
Archive Photographs
SERIES

WIDNES

Widnes from the Transporter Bridge. The square building in the foreground is St. Mary's old vicarage. West Bank School with the small spires is right of centre.

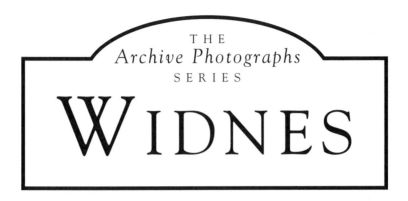

THE
Archive Photographs
SERIES

WIDNES

Compiled by
Anne Hall and the Widnes Historical Society

CHALFORD

First published 1995
Copyright © Widnes Historical Society, 1995

The Chalford Publishing Company
St Mary's Mill, Chalford,
Stroud, Gloucestershire, GL6 8NX

ISBN 0 7524 0117 3

Typesetting and origination by
The Chalford Publishing Company
Printed in Great Britain by
Redwood Books, Trowbridge

An artist's drawing of The Mersey Hotel. This hotel was also known as the Old Snig Pie House and was famous for its eel pies.

Contents

Acknowledgements

The photographs in this collection have come mainly from members and friends of the Widnes Historical Society. Mrs. Joyce Woodend, retired chairman of the Society, first made contact with the publisher and set the wheels in motion to produce this book. As the new chairman, I took over the book with the Society's members prepared to help and it is to these members, and some non-members, that I extend the Society's grateful thanks.

For photographs, information and assistance with collecting the photographs for each section, Miss Eileen Berry, Mr. George Breeden, Mrs. Muriel Brown, Mr. Albert Constable, Mr. John Dunabin, Mr. David Dwyer, Mr. Peter Hall, Mr. Stan Hall, Mr. Bob Martindale, Mrs. Cath Mullarky, Mrs. Agnes Murphy, Mr. J.A.J. Walker, Mrs. Jean Wallace and Mrs. Joyce Woodend.

For cataloguing every photograph loaned to us from the very beginning, Mr. J.A.J. Walker.

For photographs and information, Mr. G. Elliott, Mr. Alan Foster, Mr. Harper, Miss Ada Hemers, Mr. G. Howarth, Mr. Gordon Platt, Mr. T. Rolt, Mr. Bert Starkey, Mrs. Ethel Tollitt, Mrs. Gladys Valentine, Widnes Historical Society's collection.

Thanks to the *Liverpool Daily Post* and Imperial Chemical Industries for permission to use their photographs.

Thanks to Widnes Library for access to Council Records, old copies of the *Widnes Weekly News* and local reference books.

Thanks to Bob Martindale for making copies of the photographs we have used from his extensive collection.

I wish especially to thank Stan Hall for making prints from the old photographic plates of W. Hall and for help with research and Peter Hall for typing and recording text and help with research.

Anne K. Hall

With Compliments from the Smoke.

WIDNES WITH THE LID OFF, MAKES THE SUN HIDE HIS FACE

Smoke over Widnes. This is probably the most famous picture taken of Widnes when the chemical industry was in its prime.

Introduction

Most Widnesians are well aware of the fact that the development of their town has taken place over the last 150 years. History tells us of the ancient farms and hamlets which were once the homes of the scattered inhabitants of the area. There is little evidence of very early habitation in Widnes, but two Anglo-Saxon settlements existed, Ditton and Farnworth, and these two place names are still familiar to us today. The hamlet of Farnworth occupied a wooded area on higher ground about two miles from the River Mersey. Later, the villages of Farnworth, Appleton, Ditton, Cuerdley and Cronton made up Widnes.

Main highways by-passed Widnes, they headed for places where the Mersey was easier to cross, but local people had to cross the river to get to Chester and Widnes was the most convenient place. A regular ferry across the river became necessary in the twelfth century when the people of the area had to cross to Halton Castle to pay their taxes. At Widnes a sandstone promontory juts out into the river narrowing it sufficiently to make a good place for a ferry crossing. This narrow point in the river was known as the Runcorn Gap.

As the eighteenth century turned to the nineteenth, the trees, grassy areas and the river bank made the land at this spot, called West Bank, a pleasant place for visitors – as did the delights of the Snig Pie House, now the Mersey Hotel. Snig Lane led up from the river through the fields which were to change so drastically in the coming years. The extension of the Sankey-St. Helens Canal to Widnes, by means of the "new cut" and the opening of a dock, Widnes Dock, at Spike Island in 1833 by the St. Helens and Runcorn Gap Railway, made the transport of coal from the mines at St. Helens much easier.

Any pictorial record of early Widnes industry, watch making, tool making, canvas weaving, sail making and farming, has to rely on drawings or paintings, but when the chemical industry was developing in Widnes, so too was photography, enabling the pioneers in the field to record all aspects of daily life in the town. It is these images that they left which provide much of the material for this book.

The chemists and industrialists who came to Widnes – John Hutchinson, William Gossage, James Muspratt, the Hargreaves brothers, to name but few – changed the scene in Widnes completely, building factories, chimneys and acid towers. These factories created a pall of smoke and grime and the noxious smells for which Widnes became famous, or rather infamous. The rapid growth of the industries in the town led to the building, just as rapidly, of streets and streets of small houses for the workers.

The churches built in the growing community provided for the spiritual and recreational needs of the people. The Industrialists were aware of this side of their workers' lives and many of them donated to the building and furnishing of churches and helped to provide leisure facilities.

These brief paragraphs have given a glimpse of the background to the town as it grew rapidly from 1847 to the turn of the century, but yet more change was coming.

When the Leblanc process, used to produce caustic soda and the basis of Widnes' chemical industry, was challenged by a more efficient and cheaper process, the chemical industry began to decline. To alleviate the situation a large number of chemical firms, including fourteen Widnes Leblanc companies, merged to form the United Alkali Company. Some factories were closed and other operations were streamlined, even so nearly half of the town's working population was employed by the United Alkali Company.

Although Widnes was no longer the flourishing town of the late nineteenth century it remained heavily involved in the chemical industry. The United Alkali Company was not the whole story in Widnes, new industries came to Widnes bringing their own crop of chimneys, towers and strange odours. Established companies, Thomas Bolton's Copper Works for example, expanded their operations.

The demands of the First World War delayed some changes and brought about others and when the war ended the Leblanc process all but died out. United Alkali adopted the new processes it had resisted for so many years in its attempt to protect the Leblanc industry.

The Widnes which was passing is not easy for us to picture in this age committed to clean air, conservation, healthy living and safety at work. The old photographers, professional and amateur, have left us pictures of the past that show us Widnes as it used to be.

For this book we have looked for photographs which have not been used in other publications, but some, "Smoke Over Widnes", the Rugby League team and the bridges have to be included because of their importance to the town.

Our personal family connection, W. Hall, has left us many of his unique photographs which are a superb record of fifty years of people and places in Widnes and many people besides ourselves have loaned precious copies. Family photographs, treasured for years, have been taken out of albums for us to use and we are most grateful to all who have lent photographs. With the passing of time exact details of the content of the photographs become hazy, partly erased through reproduction, or lost. Although this record is not intended as a full history of Widnes, rather as a pictorial record of the last 150 years, we have endeavoured to ensure that the information given with each of the photographs is correct.

One

Bridging the Mersey

The Railway Bridge circa 1890. John Fitz Richard, 6th Baron of Halton and Widnes, established a ferry across the Mersey in 1190 and the lease for this was ultimately taken over by the London and North Western Railway Company in 1865, shortly after they had started to build their railway bridge in 1863. There are three spans of 305 ft. between castellated pylons, each wrought-iron lattice girder span is 27 ft. 9 in. deep and weighs 700 tons. This whole iron structure was built on wooden scaffolding that was knocked away on completion allowing the girders to settle onto the pylons. The foundations of the pylons are 45 ft. below the surface of the rock. For the pylons stone was used up to the high water mark and brick faced with stone above it. The approach viaduct on the Runcorn side consists of 30 arches each of 40 ft. span and 3 with 60 ft. spans. On the Widnes side the viaduct describes a sweeping curve across Widnes Marsh and has fifty-nine arches each of 40 ft. span and six of 60 ft. on to the riverbank. The viaduct arches are constructed of brick. Because of the curve a skew-arch had to be put in on the Widnes side. The evening of Thursday 21 May 1868 saw the opening of what was then the longest railway bridge in the world. The bridge was christened the Ethelfleda Bridge, after the daughter of King Alfred the Great, who crossed the river here in 916. Under the supervision of William Baker, the construction had taken five years.

Work on the Widnes Transporter Bridge began on 2 July 1902. It was built by the Widnes and Runcorn Bridge Company whose chairman was Sir John Brunner. Both Widnes Corporation and Runcorn U.D.C. subscribed to the project. The actual building work was carried out by the Arrol Bridge and Roof Co. of Glasgow. By 5 March 1903 the platforms from the shore to the tower caissons had been built. The caissons enabled the towers to be bolted into the bedrock, up to 35 ft. below the surface.

By 2 July 1903 the towers were nearly completed to their maximum height of 190 ft. above high water. The tower legs were 30 ft, apart at the base, tapering to 6 ft. 9 ins. at the top.

Early in 1904 the towers had been linked together by the main cables. There was still time for some of the workers to enjoy a game of bowls on the green at the Mersey Hotel.

JOINING UP THE CENTRES, OF WIDNES TRANSPORTE BRIDGE. 1000. FEET SPAN. 1904.

Completing the span November 1904. The centres of the great 1000 ft. span are being secured. There was 77 ft. clearance above the river at high tide.

SIR JOHN BRUNNER, M.P. OPENS THE NEW TRANSPORTER BRIDGE.

Sir John Brunner M.P. performing the opening ceremony of the Transporter Bridge on Monday 29 May 1905. The ceremony involved Sir John, who was accompanied by Lady Brunner, opening a padlock which joined two silken cords. He used a jewelled key which had the arms of Widnes and Runcorn at its top. Beneath them was an enamelled view of the Transporter and Sir John's own coat of arms. The shaft was decorated with figures in high relief symbolising the ideas of "Progress and Plenty", enriched with precious stones.

A passenger's eye view of the Transporter car's approach to Widnes. The journey took approximately two and a half minutes and would have cost you one old penny (1d), the same as to cross the river by the footpath alongside the Railway Bridge. The bottom of the car was about 12 ft. above the river at high tide and cleared the wall of the Manchester Ship Canal by 4 ft 6 ins.

After five years of operation it was evident that there was not enough traffic and a loss of £1,000 a year was being incurred by the company. Sir John Brunner paid off the company's debts and gave all his shares to Widnes Corporation in 1911. For the next two years the revenue was £5,000 per year. The Corporation then decided to overhaul the bridge, a cable drive replaced the direct electric motor drive and the car was lightened. Sir John Brunner re-opened the Bridge on 21 May 1913.

Over the years the Transporter carried a large number of distinguished visitors. Here, the approach to the Widnes end, Mersey Road, is seen decorated for the visit of King George V on 8 July 1925.

Queen Elizabeth the Queen Mother visited the Transporter in 1958. During the visit the Queen Mother also viewed models of the new road bridge and inspected the first stages of its construction.

A view of the two bridges in the 1930's when the Transporter was very busy with the beginning of the great increase in road traffic that led to the need for a new road bridge in the 1950's. A feature to note, just right of centre, is the position of the two great chimneys of Thomas Bolton's Copper Works, referred to in the Industry section.

Workers returning from Runcorn to Widnes in the evening using the footpath at the side of the Railway Bridge. The toll payable for the use of this footpath remained until the footpath was closed to the public upon the completion of the road bridge. (Photograph courtesy of the *Liverpool Daily Post*)

A reminder of the brief period when there were three bridges across the river. The new road bridge, officially opened by the Queen on 21 July 1961, has a span of 1082 ft. and the top of the arch is 280 ft. above the river. It was the first toll-free crossing of the Mersey between Widnes and Runcorn. The demolition of the Transporter Bridge cost £139,604, just under £2,000 more than it had cost to build.

Two
Industry

West Bank Viaduct in the 1900's. In 1847 John Hutchinson came to Widnes and opened his No. 1 Works, for making Soda Ash using the Leblanc process, on Spike Island. He foresaw the possibilities of the area known as Widnes Marsh and Widnes Moor for industrial development and acquired the land. He provided a dock (West Bank Dock opened in 1864) and railway system and founded what we today would call an industrial estate. After his death in 1865 more of the rural area he had acquired was used for industrial expansion.

Schooners and "Flats" in West Bank Dock *circa* 1905. Flats were flat-bottomed barges equipped with sails which enabled them to use the River Mersey as well as the canals. These vessels carried cargoes such as coal, salt and other minerals needed by industry. The masted barge *Thomas*, centre one of the three in the foreground, belonging to Abel's Sand Co. sank off Hale Head and was removed by the Mersey Docks and Harbour Board 20 June 1912. Sailing vessels similar to the schooners were still visiting West Bank Dock in the late 1950's.

The two vessels in the foreground of this view across West Bank Dock in the mid 1950's are a mud-hopper and the dredger *Robert Peel*. These were used to remove the build-up of sand and mud from the dock. Beneath the fifth coach of the passenger train is the famous skew-arch needed to allow the dock railway to pass beneath the viaduct at an angle. Local folklore maintains that this was entirely the work of a single labourer who constructed the arch after the best efforts of all the designers and engineers had failed to produce a workable design.

Horses engaged in shunting railway wagons on West Bank Dock. This practice was quite common throughout industry and in 1910 there were five horses engaged in these duties at West Bank Dock.

Hutchinson's steam locomotive *Lucy* at West Bank Dock. Built by the Avonside Engine Co. Ltd. of Bristol as Works No. 1568 in 1909, she finished her working life at Bolton's before going into preservation, initially at Birkenhead.

Steam cranes in the docks area. The driver shown on the nearer crane is John Hall who came to Widnes with the Birmingham Iron Company.

The earliest electric crane on West Bank Dock. Two steam cranes similar to those shown in the previous picture are visible to the right of the electric crane.

West Bank Dock was still in use in the late 1950's, note that the vessels are berthed three deep. The boat in the foreground belonged to the local sand and gravel company, Cooper's of West Bank.

Jimmy Knott, a long-serving Hutchinson's employee, worked on West Bank Dock. When photographed he was making an essential check on a crane-grab before unloading a boat in the early 1960's.

To manoeuvre a boat into West Bank Dock was not a straightforward operation. The vessel first had to turn in the River Mersey by steering into the slag bank and allowing the tide to bring the stern round, so entering the dock stern first. The boat enters the lock and continues stern first to its berth.

Calder and Mersey Extract Co. *circa* 1905. The company had an estate of 150 acres on Ditton Marsh. This gave the company cheap wharfage and sidings for the mainline railways. The firm made solid and liquid tanning extract, tanner's soluble oils, synthetic tanning and chrome tanning liquors. In 1924 it was the largest extract works in the United Kingdom despite having to be entirely rebuilt following a fire in 1918.

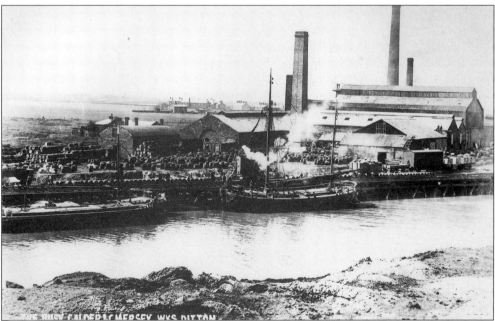

Calder and Mersey Works Quay, *circa* 1900, looking across Ditton Brook with Foundry Lane in the distance. Prior to the closure of Ditton Brook Iron Works 500-ton barges discharged cargoes of iron ore at this quay.

An aerial view of the High Speed Alloy Works, Ditton Road. In 1914 thirty-one High Speed Steel manufacturers combined to form this company to supply the Tungsten they needed. Tungsten had previously been supplied from Germany. From the bottom of the picture the factories are The Birmingham Corrugated Iron Co., High Speed Steel, Richard White's Engineers, Todd's Drums and Velvene Oils. Ditton Road is on the left, extreme left is Widnes Central Station. On the right of the picture are the lines and sidings of the LMS Railway, successor to the LNWR.

Ditton Brook Iron Works, Halebank before 1883. The works started production on 18 September 1862. After a disastrous explosion the works was demolished in about 1890. One of the two boiler houses of the works can be seen in the 1950's photograph of the Calder and Mersey Works.

The Calder and Mersey Works in the late 1950's. The building of the new road bridge can be seen beyond the railway bridge.

The New Cut, Gossage's, Spike Island and West Bank. The church on the extreme left is St. Patrick's. The rectangle of gravestones with the space is the site of old St. Mary's Church, whose fate is explained in the Churches section. The long oval body of water is a reservoir which has since been filled in. The small square of water is Widnes Dock which is still to be seen at Spike Island. Gossage's chimney is in the centre and a little back and left is the chimney of Hutchinson's No.1 Works. No smoke is coming from these chimneys as Gossage's closed in 1932 and Hutchinson's in 1919. The tower on the right, first Hutchinson's, then Gossage's offices, is now Catalyst, the museum of the Chemical Industry.

A much earlier photograph of the same area with both chimneys working full blast. The New Cut with its boats is to the left, Hutchinson's No.1 Works is in the foreground and the reservoir is to the right. Chimneys too numerous to mention follow the curve of the cut and disappear into the distance.

Two locomotives at Gossage's Soap Works, backed by barrel storage.

Thomas Bolton's new chimney, the "Topping-out" ceremony, July 1909, reported in the Weekly News as being the tallest in Widnes and the third tallest in Lancashire at 285 ft high. The cap was 12 feet high and weighed 43 tons. Bolton's 1884 chimney, seen to the right of and behind the new chimney, was built for Bolton's initial expansion of the Mersey Copper Works. This old chimney had held the title of tallest in Widnes when completed in 1884 and is the most prominent chimney in "Smoke over Widnes."

Part of the site of Thomas Bolton's Mersey Copper Works, also called the Dolphin Works, after a disastrous fire. This was the part of the works used for the electrolytic refining of copper, the bath-like structures being the lead vats used to hold the copper solution.

Manufacturing soap boxes at Gossage's Soap Works, Widnes.

Packing soap tablets at Gossage's.

Two railway workers engaged in shunting duties near Sullivan's Works in 1900. The man on the left is holding a shunter's pole, used to couple and uncouple wagons. The man on the right is pushing a barrow full of salt, presumably to aid the removal of snow and ice.

Carboy storage facility at Pilkington-Sullivan's Works, Moss Bank, Widnes. Pilkington's and Sullivan's Works, both part of the United Alkali Company, were formally merged in 1921 to form Pilkington-Sullivan's, by which name they continued to be known after the formation of ICI in 1926. The glass carboys were used to transport the highly corrosive acid from Widnes to many places. They were protected from damage by iron cages well packed with straw.

Industry along the Sankey-St. Helens Canal, the Widnes "new cut", 1920. The factories from left to right are Gaskell-Deacon, Alumina, Muspratt's, Pilkington's and Sullivan's. All of these, with the exception of Alumina, became part of ICI.

Mersey Flats in the Sankey-St. Helens Canal before the First World War. The fully-laden flat at the right of the picture is sitting very low in the water.

ICI Muspratt Works 1950. Workers breaking up black ash (from fusing coke, salt-cake and limestone) after removing it from a revolver, a large rotating kiln. By this time the black ash was only used to produce Sodium Sulphide. In the Leblanc process the black ash was placed in water in large vats, and the resulting liquor causticized using slaked lime.

Pyrites burners, Pilkington's Works 1900. These long rows of ovens were an essential feature of factories using the Leblanc process. The pyrites was roasted to release sulphur dioxide which was used to produce vitriol (concentrated sulphuric acid) and thence sodium sulphate (salt-cake) and ultimately caustic soda.

Greenbank Staff in 1924 with a high percentage of women workers. Their "Red Heart" brand of caustic soda and bleaching powder became well known. In 1921 the small packaging department moved from St. Helens to Pilkington-Sullivan's Works in Widnes.

United Alkali Company's Commer wagon in 1924 decorated and displaying products made at the Greenbank Works, Widnes.

Interior of UAC Power House, West Bank, 1920. In 1920 the United Alkali Company established a central power station at West Bank Dock. Initially the new power station supplied Pilkington-Sullivan Works, but eventually all the factories owned by UAC drew their power from it. C.P. Hall is sixth from the front in the centre row of workers.

The building of J.H. Dennis' Cornubia Works, 1883. Mildew was severely affecting the French vineyards in the 1880's, copper salts had proved very effective against mildew and demand for copper sulphate increased. To meet this demand, James Hawke Dennis established his Cornubia Works.

Workers at J.H. Dennis' Cornubia Works.

Gaskell-Deacon Processmen and Foremen *circa* 1890.

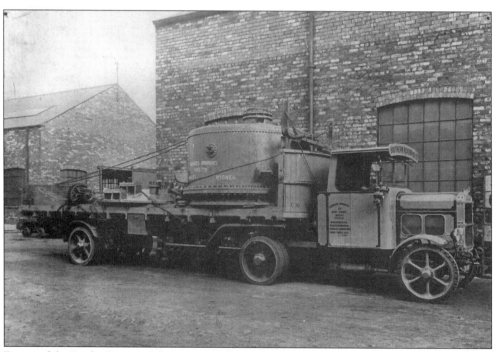

Destined for Poole, Dorset. A large casting leaves Widnes Foundry in 1925.

A five-way valve produced by Widnes Foundry in 1900 for the pipeline bringing water from North Wales to Liverpool.

Towers' Glass *circa* 1918. Glassblowers at their workbenches engaged in glass blowing and calibration of completed glassware. The founder of the firm, John William Towers, was originally employed in the laboratories of Hutchinson's Chemical Works. However his ambitious nature led him to desire a business of his own, and so he turned a profitable hobby, that of making microscope slides, into a business that manufactured and sold all kinds of chemical apparatus.

The Hurter laboratory on Waterloo Road was founded in 1891 by Ferdinand Hurter, a Swiss chemist who came to Widnes in 1867. The building with the bay-window overlooking the signal-box was originally the gatekeeper's lodge of the Gaskell-Deacon Works, and later became part of the laboratory. The building on the far end of the row was the Gaskell-Deacon Baths, the first Public Baths in Widnes.

James Hargreaves 1834–1915. A pioneer of the Widnes chemical industry, Hargreaves was a prolific inventor and made significant contributions to the soap, alkali, metallurgical and electrochemical industries. He virtually anticipated the invention of the Diesel engine with his thermo engine and was one of the first to propose the use of gaseous chlorine for the treatment of sewage.

Three
Transport

Unusually for a town of its size Widnes never had any street tramways, but early in the century the need was felt for some form of local transport. After a trial period of two months in 1906 using a motorbus provided by a Burnley company, followed by further operation with another hired vehicle, Widnes Corporation purchased its own bus fleet, four covered top Commers, in 1909. In April they commenced daily services linking the Transporter Bridge with the town centre and Peel House Lane, later extending to Halton View, Farnworth, Lunt's Heath and, infrequently, Rainhill. Halton Transport, as the Corporation's service is now known, continues to provide passenger transport across the Borough. The first bus used in Widnes, a Critchley-Norris, is pictured above whilst on trial.

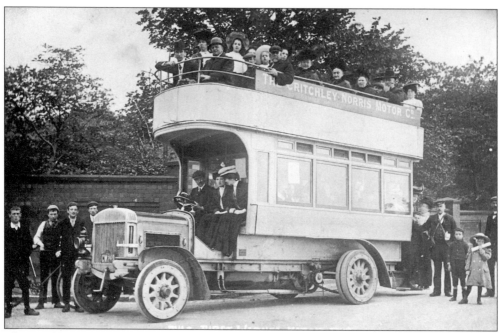

The Crichley-Norris on a pleasure trip at Lunt's Heath whilst on trial.

One of the Widnes Commers in Victoria Square complete with mudguards outside the wheels.

Three of Widnes' four Commer buses delivered new in 1909. These were the first covered-top buses in England, if not the World.

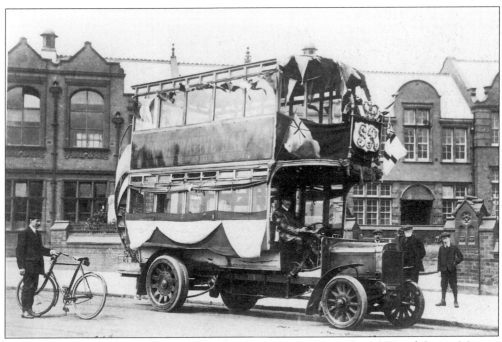

A Widnes Corporation bus decorated for the Coronation of King George V and Queen Mary in 1911. Note the appearance of an advertisement on the upper panels of the bus. This one advertising the Co-operative Hall, "The Widnes Family Resort".

A Bus waiting at the Transporter Bridge for the arrival of the Transporter Car from Runcorn.

Thornycroft steam wagon and trailer in Ditton Road, turning on to the approach road to Widnes Central Station.

A 5 ton Commer motor lorry of the United Alkali Company loaded with carboys.

A United Alkali Company Sentinel steam wagon and trailer, well laden with 135 carboys.

The junction of Derby Road, Peel House Lane and Farnworth Street at the turn of the century when the horse-drawn van and handcart were the most common forms of home delivery.

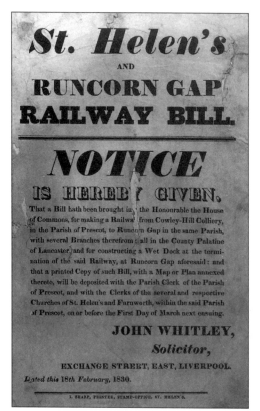

A notice from 1830 advising the population of the presentation in the House of Commons of a Bill for the construction of the St. Helens and Runcorn Gap Railway. The line opened in 1833 and just failed to make it to its 150th. Anniversary, being closed as a through route in 1981.

Building Farnworth Station in 1872. This station was on the Cheshire Lines Committee route from Manchester to Liverpool. The CLC was jointly owned by the Manchester, Sheffield & Lincolnshire (later the Great Central), Midland and Great Northern Railways who desired access to the lucrative traffic to and from Liverpool over their own lines, rather than having to hand trains over to the LNWR.

Farnworth station *circa* 1905. The approaching train is one belonging to the Midland Railway.

Tanhouse Lane station in the late 1950's. Located on the now closed Widnes loop-line, this station was built on land donated by Messrs. Pilkington's. The loop-line ran from Widnes East Junction to Hough Green and was jointly owned by the MSLR and the MR. Although effectively a part of the CLC system the GNR refused to allow the loop-line's inclusion in the CLC, so it remained the property of the other two and was referred to as the Sheffield and Midland Joint.

An express passenger train passing through Farnworth station in 1907. The CLC was unusual, even amongst joint lines, in that although it owned passenger carriages and goods wagons, it had no locomotives of its own, instead the Great Central provided the motive power for the CLC's internal services and each company provided the power for trains to destinations on their own networks. In this case the locomotive is one belonging to the Great Central Railway.

Four
Street Scenes

Mersey Road, West Bank. At the time of this photograph West Bank was well served by shops. In this stretch of the road Martin's Bank is on the right hand side on the corner of Irwell Street with a grocers on the opposite corner, Davis Dyers and a watchmakers can be identified on the original photograph, together with other shops further away. There was a much larger community in West Bank when the industries of the area, Gossage's, Hutchinson's etc. were flourishing.

Waterloo Road curves round from Mersey Road, past the Spike Island area, heading for Victoria Road and the Town Hall square.

Victoria Road was the continuation of Waterloo Road which headed for the area which had become the town centre. Bridges carried the railways over Victoria Road which was lined with shops. The first shop on the right is G. Naylor's, the hairdresser featured in the next picture.

G. Naylor, hairdresser with his young assistant.

Widnes Road carried on through town from Victoria Square. These buildings are still recognisable today, although the traders have changed. After the provision and flour warehouse the small notice reads "Motor repairs and accessories". The next corner is The Public Benefit Boot Co. Ltd. and the next corner is "——— Cheap Clothing Mart", next to the Pawn Brokers, a sign of the times. The premises of Lewis and Calvert Ltd. facing the camera have been replaced by newer buildings.

Looking down on Victoria Road from St. Paul's tower we see buildings which are still there today, but in different hands. The Police Station, opposite the Library and most of the chimneys have gone, only Bolton's chimney remains at the time of writing. Boots Cash Dispensing Chemists is the shop on the corner. The shop with the veranda is Frank Johnson's Tailors. The large square roofed building was the Victoria Road Chapel, now the Queens Hall.

Frank Johnson the Tailor advertised in the local cinemas and this is a print from one of his advertising slides. Mussolini, Hitler, Stalin and Gandhi are the wearers of the shirts referred to in the advert.

The old Appleton Quarry in 1889. The quarry has now been filled-in, but the wall still stands round St. Bede's Church which still faithfully serves the local community.

Appleton Village in winter.

Birchfield Road from the Bridle Path in the Farnworth area of Widnes.

YE OLDE TYME BLACK HORSE, FARNWORTH.

The old Black Horse, Farnworth, at the top end of Birchfield Road which was demolished and a new Hotel built on the site.

The new Black Horse Hotel, which replaced the one shown above.

Halton View Road looking towards the Castle Hotel. St. Ambrose Church is on the right. The large chimney-like structure is in fact a sewer vent of which there were several around the town. One still survives on Mill Brow, near to where Halton View Road crosses the new by-pass.

Walter Winn stands at the door of his newsagents and general stores in Latham Street, at the Halton View end of Albert Road.

Houses in Cross Street, at the top end of Albert Road, with the householders dressed and posed for their photograph.

Five
Life and Times

The Widnes Star Novelty Prize Jazz Band was formed by a group of about one hundred men who were unemployed in the late twenties and early thirties. Their aim was to brighten their own and their neighbours' lives in the time of the depression. The band became very well known and broadcast from the BBC Manchester studio in May 1932. A sound film recording of the band was made in the yard of the Technical School.

A popular hobby with many Widnes men was pigeon racing, some races going to the continent. This group of Pigeon-fanciers came from the Moss Bank area.

A treat for the children in the early years of this century was the visit of the rag and bone man with his round-about. The residents of Christie Street are out in force with their youngest children eager to enjoy a ride.

Mr. Caufield and his sixteen grandchildren. Named by the residents "King of Moss Bank", Mr. Caufield was a great character, always ready to support members of the community with help and advice.

The "back-entry" to a house was a feature of much of the terraced housing in Widnes, here G. Oultram and his father stand in the back-entry to their house in Warrington Road, opposite St. Ambrose Road – sharing the picture with some ducks.

This group of pensioners photographed on the prom at West Bank have successfully survived the hazards of living and working in the chemical industry in Widnes. Their ages total 2225, so they had all reached their seventies.

Royal London Staff Outing to Blackpool, 26 June 1930. The staff or works outing was a popular feature of the working year and was not complete without having a, sometimes rather formal, photograph taken as a reminder of the occasion.

A group of cheerful Woolworth's employees photographed in 1948. On the back row left to right Mary Shannon, Brenda Morris, Vera Meadon and Peggy Sadler. Front row Audrey Stacey, Jean Ashton and one unknown.

Many works had their teams to represent them at various sports. The writing on the ball proclaims that this is Sullivan's football team in the early years of this century.

"The Kennels" at Hough Green. The house was so named because the dogs for the Waterloo Cup hare-coursing event had been kept there. Later the Hunt family moved to the house and took in laundry from the big houses in Liverpool. In this 1910 scene, Ada Hunt is on the extreme right, she is also in the photograph of St. Michael's Infants. The house still stands amongst new buildings in Hough Green Road.

A family connection of the Hunt's, Margaret Hall, with her young son, feeds the hens at their house in Halton View which used to stand opposite the Castle Hotel.

This group of young ladies formed the "Sewing Band" under the guidance of Mrs. Lineker (Emily Moore). They were connected with St. Ambrose Church, Halton View, and were photographed in about 1919.

Two young people proud of their bikes in 1921, their dress somewhat formal for leisure by our standards.

J.H. Breeden aged 4 and his older brother aged 5 outside their home in Mill Lane.

Church Street Farnworth, now called Farnworth Street, showing the old Post Office. Mr. W. Jones is in the shop doorway.

The pony and trap used by the Davies family in 1900. From the left George Davies, Frank (his son), Mr. Verity, Mrs. Davies and Mrs. Verity.

A different form of pleasure transport was the charabanc. Blackpool was the destination for the employees of J.W. Towers. The essential photograph of the occasion was taken before the start of the journey to Blackpool.

Britain was still at war in 1917, but life still went on at home. May was the time for new Mayors to take office and here we see the new Mayor, Cllr. G. Davies attending a service at Victoria Road Chapel. He is preceded by the mace-bearer who appears in several other pictures in this book.

The Coronation in 1911 of King George V and Queen Mary was commemorated with the ceremonial planting of a tree in Victoria Park. It was planted near the Gladstone fountain and close to a tree planted for the Coronation of King Edward VII. The Mayor, Cllr. F. Neill planted the tree and was presented with a silver cup as a memento by Cllr. Edwin Wood, the chairman of the Parks and Cemeteries Committee.

Outside the Everite Works on Derby Road a float sets off for the procession to celebrate the 1951 Festival of Britain.

Another reason for a procession and a picnic was Co-op Day. At the time this photograph was taken in 1919 the Runcorn and Widnes Co-operative Society was a flourishing part of trade in the two towns.

Widnes had a reputation for the impressive style of its decorations and celebrations of great occasions. For Queen Victoria's Diamond Jubilee in 1894 and for the visit of King George V and Queen Mary in 1913 triumphal arches were built in the town. The one shown here was the arch built in Halton View for the latter occasion. It went from the Castle Hotel right across the road and the King and Queen drove through the arch on their way to the Town Hall. St. Ambrose Church is seen through the arch. Note the little girl at left is in bare feet. The procession passing through the arch is St. Ambrose Sunday School.

King George V and Queen Mary being greeted by civic dignitaries and other officials at the Town Hall on 7 July 1913.

King George V visited Widnes again on 8 July 1925. He was greeted in Victoria Square by several bands and choirs and a peal from St. Paul's bells. From the square the King drove to West Bank and crossed the river by the Transporter Bridge.

A cheery group of young ladies on their way to the Rose Queen festivities of *circa* 1936. The young lady with her sash on the opposite way is Marjorie Latham.

Mrs. Maggie Wilkinson of the Golden Bowl pub. Mrs. Wilkinson was very well known to the Moss Bank community and to the workers from the ICI factories in the area. The Golden Bowl was demolished some years ago.

St. Marie's Band 1908. St. Marie's R.C. Church in Lugsdale Road served the Newtown area. There were many Irish families in the hastily built streets of houses for chemical workers. St. Marie's Church was opened in 1862 to serve their needs. The Bandsmen are: (back row) Connor, -?-, Mooney, -?-, -?-, -?-, Chris Moran. Second row: -?-, Coleman, McGuire, Waters, -?-, Fitzgerald. Front row: Mark Flanagan, -?-, H. Harrison, Jim Redmond, -?-, -?-, Billy Burke. Boy in front is Young Brady.

The River Mersey and West Bank Promenade at high tide. A pleasant mid-day scene at the turn of the century, with some locals sunning themselves. A large number of boats are lying in the river. These include several fishing smacks, some Mersey flats, a tug and a topsail schooner.

Widnes Promenade. Looking down from the Transporter Landing on a very busy day.

E. Farr's Ice Cream sales cart in West Bank 1933.

A. Cooper's lemonade delivery cart in the twenties. A. Cooper of West Bank manufactured his own Lemonade and minerals. The cart was a familiar sight in Widnes.

Vicarage Garden Party *circa* 1912. Church activities were an important part of local life and the vicarage was often the venue for a Garden Party as here at St. Ambrose Vicarage. Hats were essential wear for ladies attending such an occasion, including the Church Army sister.

Rose Queen, St. Ambrose *circa* 1931. Some years later and hats are still in vogue for these occasions, but styles have changed, even for the Church Army sister (Sister Lever). There seems to be a fashion hitch here – two ladies wearing the same dress!

Six

School Days

St. Michael's C. of E. Infants' class *circa* 1895. The oldest school in Widnes was Farnworth Grammar School, founded in 1577 and endowed by William Smythe, Bishop of Lincoln and a native of Widnes. This foundation continued into the twentieth century. Education for other children fell to the churches. Before the formation of the School Board in 1874, Widnes had two National Schools, St. Mary's and Farnworth; three Roman Catholic Schools, St. Marie's, St. Bede's and St. Patrick's; and three Wesleyan Day Schools at Ditton, Moss Bank and Sutton's Lane. In 1902 the School Board was replaced by Widnes Education Committee. In this picture Ada Hunt is next but one to the teacher on the left.

Enoch Brown and Mrs. Brown 1901. Henry Enoch Brown was master of Farnworth Boys School for forty-three years. He was photographed with his wife Rachel on his retirement in 1901.

Dinner-time at Farnworth Schools. Boys and girls running home for dinner along School Lane, now re-named Pit Lane.

Marbles Derby Day at Farnworth school 1910. The building on the right is the old school, now demolished. Many people who attended Farnworth School well remember this building and the iron staircase that led to the upper floor.

The Farnworth Grammar School building in Peel House Lane, opened in 1884. The grammar school for boys was housed here until insufficient funds and a decline in the number of pupils caused its closure in 1905. The school was transferred to the Widnes Secondary School, in the Technical School building, until 1931 when the Wade Deacon Grammar School opened.

TERMS

AND

REGULATIONS

RESPECTING

Farnworth School,

Is determined by the TRUSTEES at a General Meeting convened for that Purpose, July 25th, 1805.

RESOLVED,

That each Scholar shall pay, for Entrance, 2 6

II.

For Reading English,   5 0 *per Quarter.*
For Writing,   7 6 ditto.
For Accounts,   10 6 ditto.

III.

For Drawing at Shrovetide, commonly called Cock Money,   1 0
For Fire Money,   1 6
For Feast Money, at Christmas,   1 0

☞ Boys belonging to the Chapelry, who learn Grammar only, are FREE; and Boys who can read well in the Testament, so as to be capable of learning Grammar, to be also FREE in respect of their reading.

HOLIDAYS TO BE KEPT.

On WEDNESDAY and SATURDAY Afternoon's.
At SHROVETIDE,   one Week.
—— EASTER,   one Week.
—— WHITSUNTIDE,   one Week.
—— FARNWORTH WAKE,   one Week.
—— CHRISTMAS,   one Month.

TRUSTEES.

The Minister of Farnworth.	*John Watkins, Esq. for Ditton.*
Peter Robinson and } *for Bold*	*John Leigh, Esq. for Cronton.*
Thomas Roughsedge, }	*David Claughton, Gent. for Sankey.*
Samuel Woolrich and } *for Widnes.*	*John Harrison, for Cuerdley.*
Thos. Kidd, Gentlemen, }	*Richard Woodward, for Penketh.*

10

Terms and Regulations for Farnworth School.

THE DOOR UNLOCKED, 10th September, 1931

by Sir Henry Wade Deacon, accompanied by the Chairman of the Governors, Mr. A. E. Calvert.

The door unlocked, 10 September 1931. The official opening of Wade Deacon Grammar School by Sir Henry Wade Deacon, accompanied by Mr. A.E. Calvert, chairman of governors.

A Wade Deacon School occasion. Left to right: Doctor Bailey, Mr. Herbert Green (headmaster), Dr. Porterfield, Mr. A.E. Calvert. Dr. Jones (Medical Officer) and one unknown.

Wade Deacon Grammar School Speech Day 1946. Bishop Martin of Liverpool being greeted by the Head Boy for 1945/6, John Hall, the Head Girl, Jean Laws (now Mrs. Gravett) and the headmaster, Herbert Green.

The new Wade Deacon Grammar School opened in 1931.

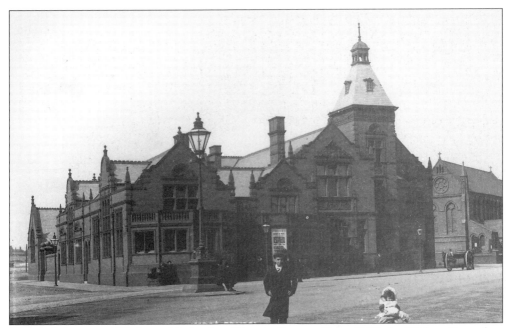

Widnes Library and Technical School in Victoria Square. From 1905 the Widnes Secondary School was housed in the Technical School building.

Widnes Secondary School Sports 1913. A fine array of trophies is waiting to be presented.

Widnes Secondary School. Hockey club 1st. Team in the early 1920's.

St. Michael's C. of E. Junior School in the 1890's.

St. Bede's Infants in 1912.

Warrington Road School 1937. The headmaster, Mr. Hector Ireland, watches as a tree is planted on St. Ambrose field to commemorate the Coronation of King George VI and Queen Elizabeth. The field was behind the school and was sold to the Education Authority after the war. Waiting his turn, fifth in line in the light coat is Stan Hall.

Empire Day at Warrington Road School in about 1907. The pupils were dressed to represent the countries of the Empire. Fourth from the left, dressed as India is Margaret Isherwood, later Hall, her looks cast her for this part. Empire Day was celebrated by all schools on 28 May.

The Court of Queen Summergold in 1917. All schools had their seasonal fetes and celebrations, not just church schools. This Summer celebration was at Warrington Road. Reading, writing, arithmetic and other academic subjects were very important and these other events were a welcome change from the formal teaching of the early part of this century.

Seven

Churches
and Church Life

St. Luke's Church Farnworth. The Bold Chapel can be seen in the centre of this picture taken from the back of the church. St. Luke's is the oldest church in Widnes, dating from around 1180. When Widnes was a flourishing chemical town there was much church building. Sadly with the decline of the chemical industry and church-going in general, some of these buildings have been demolished or put to another use.

Nevertheless Widnes still has some excellent churches in St. Ambrose, St. Bede's, St. Marie's, St. Mary's, St. Patrick's, St. Paul's, both St. Michael's, Farnworth Methodist Church and the Baptist Church. There are also the newer churches including, St. Basil's, St. John's, St. John Fisher, St. Pius X, St. Raphael's and the new Peel House Lane Methodist Church. The activities connected with the churches formed the entertainment available to Widnesians until the era of the "wireless", film and television.

Interior of St. Luke's Church Farnworth before the chandeliers were inverted when converted from gas to electricity.

> ## In FARNWORTH CHURCH,
> On *Tuesday* the 25th *June* 1771, will be perform'd,
> By a numerous Band of *Vocal* and *Instrumental Musicians*, collected from different parts of the country,
>
> ## The Sacred ORATORIO of the
> # MESSIAH.
> Set to Music by *George Frederick Handel*, Esq.
>
> The Choruses will be accompanied with Drums, Trumpets, Violins, Hautboys, Tenor Violins, Violoncellos, Bassoons, &c.
>
> The doors to be opened at ten o'clock, and the performance to begin exactly at eleven.
>
> TICKETS at 1s. and Books of the Oratorio at 3d. each, to be had at Widow *Shaw's* and Mr. *Rawson's*, in *Farnworth*; Mr. *Peter Taylor's*, at *Sankey* Chapel; Mr. *John Woods*, in *St. Hellens*; and Mr. *Thomas Sephton's*, and *James May's*, in *Prescot*.

Performance of Handel's *Messiah* advertised to take place in Farnworth Church in 1771.

St. Bede's Church in Appleton. There was a Catholic community in the area long before St. Bede's was built. The protection given to Priests by important Catholic families ensured the continuance of the Roman Catholic faith in Widnes. St. Bede's was opened and consecrated in 1847, Roman Catholics travelled from all over South Lancashire to attend the opening service, paying for tickets. Those arriving by train were met at Rainhill station by horse-drawn vehicles.

St. Bede's was a large flourishing parish, as this picture of St. Bede's Sunday School shows.

Farnworth Village. The large open area shows the essentially rural character of Farnworth in the early 1900's. Farnworth Wesleyan Chapel, opened on Sunday 29 May 1892 can be seen in the middle distance. The pulpit in the chapel came from Runcorn Parish Church. This chapel replaced one opened in 1849.

Widnes Wesleyan Methodist Circuit Rally.

Wesley Church, Peel House Lane, brand new in 1905, but now demolished and replaced by the new Trinity Methodist Church on the same site.

The interior of Victoria Road Wesleyan Chapel as it was when used for worship. It was sold to Widnes Borough Council and is now the Queens Hall.

Frederick Street Primitive Methodist Church, opened in 1905 but no longer in existence.

The Salvation Army Hall which was opened on 21 November 1908, General Booth is shown in the inset on a rare visit to Widnes. The Widnes Corps was formed in 1881. A group of them, including four women, found themselves imprisoned for asserting their right to meet publicly in Victoria Square. Strong public support for their cause forced the authorities to allow them to meet in the square.

Widnes Baptist Church Sunday School, 1920's.

Milton Congregational Church and Hall. The hall still stands in Widnes Road but the church has gone.

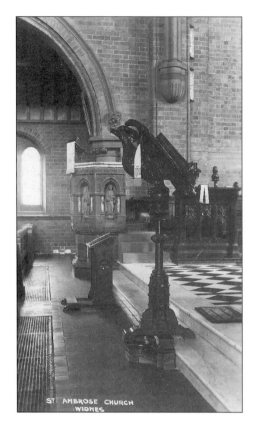

St. Ambrose Church, Halton View. The church was opened in 1881 but was not consecrated until December 1883 when the debt on the building was cleared.

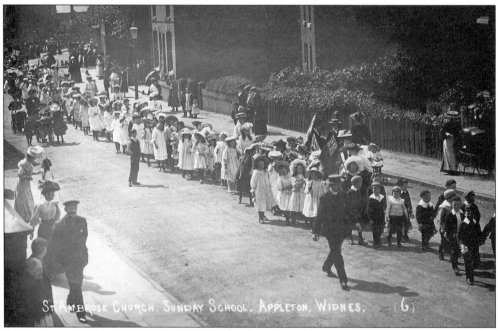

St. Ambrose Sunday School Treat, 1907. The Rev. H. P. Hiscoke accompanies the procession to Knowles' field at Cuerdley. The children are all carrying cups.

St. Ambrose Treat, 1927. Times change and in the case of St Ambrose's Sunday School Treat fashions have changed – but not for the Church Army Sister! Other things stay the same; the venue was still the field of Mr. Knowles and the children still carry their own cups.

Corpus Christi Celebration at St. Marie's, 1923. This was an important celebration for Roman Catholics and a good reason for a procession. The people are led by the Rev. Father Barry along Lugsdale Road.

Church Rose Queen Group in 1938. The retiring queen wearing the crown is Betty Williams and the Queen-elect, wearing the head-dress with a star, is Joan Standen. The Rose Queen Festival was a great occasion in church life between the wars and some churches have retained or revived this event.

A Rose Queen of 1932. Miss Eunice Barton with two young attendants.

The old St. Mary's Church, West Bank. The nave of the church was opened in 1858, but the tower, spire and chancel of the original plan were never built. Unfortunately this church, sometimes known as Widnes Dock Church, was built on chemical waste. By 1901 cracks had appeared and the walls bulged outwards because the foundations were not secure and the church was closed.

The new St. Mary's Church, West Bank. This much larger building replaced the old St. Mary's and was opened in 1910, A fine sandstone building, it was built on a site near the new promenade and could seat 770 people. Forty-two houses were removed to make way for the church.

St. Michael's C. of E. Church, Ditchfield Road. The church records tell us that the building was opened in 1870 and consecrated in 1874 when the debt on the building was cleared. The other St. Michael's Church is in St. Michael's Road and is a Roman Catholic church.

The congregation leaving St. Paul's Church after the dedication of the bells. The church was opened in 1884. The tower was built some years later and opened on 20 September 1906. The bells were dedicated in 1907.

Members of St. Paul's "Pleasant Sunday Afternoon" group who visited local places of interest.

A UNIQUE PHOTO. OF WIDNES TOWN HALL. ST PAULS CHURCH & TECHNICAL SCHOOL

St. Paul's Church after the completion of the tower from an unusual viewpoint, probably just outside the "Grapes" public house. This view is not possible today because of the buildings that now stand on Widnes Road.

St. Ambrose Girls' Friendly Society, 1915. All denominations had organisations for their young people. G.F.S., the Scout and Guide movement, the Boys' Brigade and others. Until 1902 the Widnes district of the G.F.S. was a section of the Childwall Branch. On 1 July 1902 the Widnes Branch was formed, consisting of Ditton St. Michael's, St. Mary's and St. Ambrose.

St. Michael's Guides 1951. Many of the church organisations are still going strong having updated their image to maintain their appeal to young people.

Eight
War and Peace

War Memorial (A), Widnes.

The Widnes War Memorial in Victoria Park was unveiled by Lord Derby on 28 September 1921. Listed on the Memorial are the names of the 818 Widnes men who were killed in the 1914–18 war. After the Second World War the names of the 289 men and women who gave their lives in that conflict were added.

A Recruiting Rally at West Bank, 2 October 1915. Widnes men responded to the call to arms, although the chemical industry was employing more people in Widnes because of the increased production needed for the war effort.

Bomb damage in Marsh Hall Road and Windermere Street after the air-raid of 21 October 1941. Because of the chemical industry, Widnes expected to be a target for air raids. The town's children were evacuated to Blackpool in September 1939, but most returned to Widnes in the Autumn.

After the funeral service of Sgt. J. Burgess at St. Ambrose Church. Sgt. Burgess' name can be found on the War Memorial.

A stockpile of Gas Shells at Sullivan's Works. During the First World War, Sullivan's was the only Widnes firm making phosgene. Other chemical factories in the town made explosives and the foundries also made steel hut sections, railway sleepers, steelmasts for wireless telegraphs and munitions.

H.M.S. *Widnes*. This mine sweeper has an interesting history. A ship of the second group of "Hunt" class mine sweepers she was launched on 28 June 1918. During the Second World War she served in the Mediterranean, but had to be beached after an air attack at Suda Bay, Crete. She was salvaged by the Germans and served for them as Patrol Vessel Uj. 2109 and was sunk in Kalymnos Harbour by gunfire from H.M.S. *Jervis* and H.M.S. *Penn* on 17 October 1943.

Private Charles Hunt after he had joined the Army in 1914.

The Mayor of Widnes, Councillor Edwin Wood at the laying of the foundation stone of the Widnes War Memorial. He was accompanied by the deputy Mayor, Councillor Wareing. The stone was laid on 28 July 1920.

The procession en route to the unveiling of the Widnes War Memorial in Victoria Park on 28 September 1921.

Post-war AFS (Auxilliary Fire Service) in training. Station Officer R. Morrison instructs the men on the use of a small portable pump. Because of the "Cold War" situation after the Second World War the service was carried on and the men kept in training.

St. Bede's War Memorial 1920.

St. Ambrose Church, Widnes

Stained-glass window in St. Ambrose Church. The window depicts St. Boniface, Apostle to Germany 680–754, who came from England. This window was given by German Prisoners of War, from Penketh Hostel, who attended services at St. Ambrose Church "in grateful memory of services held here". The window was dedicated on 3 May 1947.

The German Prisoners of War from Penketh Hostel after the service of dedication for the window. In the photograph are Clifford Martin, Bishop of Liverpool, Mrs. Bankes, and behind her the Rev. Joseph Hignett Bankes, Vicar of St. Ambrose. To the right of the photo are the Mayor and Mayoress of Widnes.

Peace Day showing the junction of Lugsdale Road and Moon Street. The wall on the right belongs to the Vine Site of Orr's Zinc White Ltd.

Peace was celebrated in Widnes on Saturday 19 July 1919. Through the Sunday Schools a treat was organized for over 10,000 school children. The children assembled in Victoria Square, sang *God Save The King* and processed to Victoria Park for tea and games. In the evening there was a huge bonfire between Widnes Road and Kingsway, which was wasteland in 1919.

Nine
Sport and Leisure

Sport played an important part in the leisure activities of the town; churches, works, public houses and districts all had their various sports teams for cricket, athletics, football, both types of rugby and virtually any other sport, indoor or outdoor, you care to name. The most famous sports team in the town is its Rugby League team. Widnes Rugby League Football Club began in 1873 as the Farnworth and Appleton Football Club, the name changing to Widnes two years later. In 1895 Widnes, together with nineteen other clubs, resigned from the Rugby Football Union in a dispute over paying players the money they lost from work whilst playing for the team. They formed the Northern Rugby Football Union. The NRFU changed its name to the now well known Rugby Football League in 1922.

Widnes Rugby League team at Wembley in 1950 being presented to the Prime Minister, Mr. Clement Atlee. The captain, T. Sale, introduces the team, from left to right, Fred Leigh, C. Wilcox, R. Bond, R. Rowbotham, H. "Tich" Anderson, J. Fleming. On this visit to Wembley Widnes were beaten by Warrington.

The I.C.I. Junior Rugby League team in 1938.

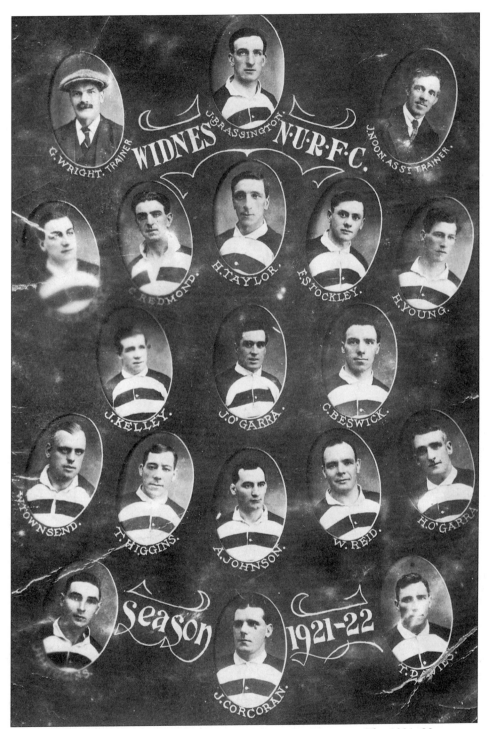

Widnes Northern Union Rugby Football Club of the 1921–22 season. The 1921–22 season was the last for the Northern Rugby Football Union, the name was changed to the Rugby Football League in June 1922. The first name in the second row reads Gregory and J. Higgins is the first name on the bottom row.

Farnworth Rugby Football Club, 1916.

The Widnes Marathon, 1909, dated from the photograph. The race was run from Earlestown to Widnes and the winner, Rimmer, is marked with a cross.

A memorable group of runners at Lowerhouse Lane *circa* 1908. The runner on the left is Rimmer who appears in the preceding photograph. Running was a popular sport and enthusiasts trained on Cuerdley and Ditton Marsh.

A walking "match" *circa* 1895. Captioned by the photographer in about 1920 as being twenty-five years ago. We can also have an idea of the date of the original photograph because the policeman seen at the right also appears in the photograph from the last Farnworth sports (Page 113). His number can be read in both photographs, No. 1193.

A Walking Match, circa 1894, photographed at Hough Green Bowling Club. A well known athlete of the time, Downer, is marked with an 'X'. He is mentioned in the *Weekly News* of 1894 as giving the winner a good race.

Hough Green Cricket Club photographed on 18 July 1903.

Hough Green Golf Club, 1922. The clubhouse is still in Ditchfield Road and is now known as Hough Green Recreation Club.

The ladies of Hough Green Cricket Club in 1900.

The members of Lane Tennis Club in the 1930's. The club is still in existence off Coroner's Lane.

The last Widnes Sports to be held at Farnworth, 1895. The Widnes Athletic Club Sports had been held on the show field at Farnworth since 1868, the event replacing Farnworth Wakes which were last held in 1865. The sports drew class runners from all over the country because of the high standard of competition and excellent prizes. Most of the races were handicap races and this gave rise to occasional bouts of skulduggery. The *Weekly News*, in its report of the 1894 sports, tells us that a professional runner, hoping to avoid being handicapped, gave a false name. He was spotted by two other competitors as being a professional, who reported him, but not before he had run in a race where he dead-heated for first place. He was banned from taking any further part in the sports. Farnworth was used for the last time in 1895. The following year the sports were held at the Lowerhouse Lane ground of Widnes Football Club, where they continued to flourish. We read that "Widnes Sports are amongst the best, if not the best, in the North-West". As many as 5,000 people attended the sports on the Saturday, and special trains were run from both Liverpool and Manchester for people who wished to join the locals at the sports.

Muspratt's Cricket and Football Teams for the 1926/27 season. Both teams were cup-winners that season.

Valentine lands in Widnes 28 July 1911. Mr. Valentine was attempting a flight round England and landed in a field at Upper House Farm, near the Ball o' Ditton. He had left Carlisle at 7 o'clock that morning and was accommodated for the night at Upper House.

The Judges of the Widnes Horticultural Society Show, 1912.

The Co-optimists at the Alexandra Theatre in 1926. This group of Co-operative Society workers formed a dance troupe and entertained locally. Here they are performing at the Mayor's "At Home" at the Alexandra Theatre. Names known are Lily Houghton, fourth from left and Marjorie Hosker, second from right.

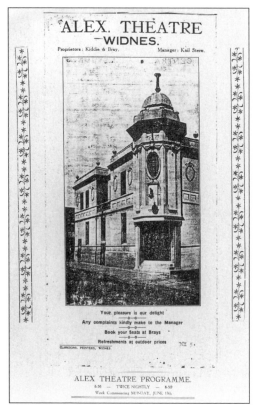

The Alexandra Theatre, Widnes. The oldest theatre in the town, it was burnt down in the 1940's

Six charabancs were needed for this outing *circa* 1920.

Hough Green May Queen, 1923. Left to right: Hilda Kay (the May Queen), Margaret Lewis (the retiring queen) and Cecil Tennison is the small boy. The cart is standing in Ash Lane.

St. Michael's June Fair, 1937. Mrs McCausland crowned the new Rose Queen, Alice Harrison. The vicar was the Rev. F.M.B. Carr. Arthur Reeves is the jester.

Ditton Band 1887. The Brass Band was a very popular form of entertainment and many Widnes men devoted their leisure hours to playing in one.

Mount Pleasant, Peel House Lane *circa* 1904. Mrs. W. Cooper and her son Thomas Cooper in the garden at Mount Pleasant. The family business was Cooper's Sand and Gravel of West Bank.

Model boat, used in the West Bank model boat races.

C.P. Hall tuning a Crystal Set in the 1920's. The crystal set was the herald of change in the leisure scene, signalling the age of radio, and later, television.

Ten

Places and Personalities from the Past

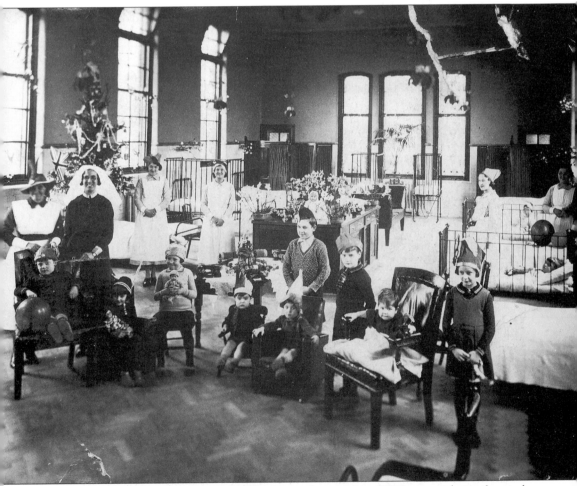

Crow Wood Hospital, Christmas 1936. The hospital opened in 1893 as an isolation hospital. The hospital treated more typhoid cases than scarlet fever cases in the1890's. In November of 1918 the hospital was busy with especially severe cases of influenza.

The Rev. J. Wright-Williams, Vicar of St. Mary's, Widnes from 1879 to 1888 and of St. Luke's, Farnworth from 1892 to 1917. He realised that Widnes would develop towards the present town centre and secured the site for St. Paul's Church. He also set in motion the 1894–5 restoration of St. Luke's, the aim being to "restore the ancient features of the church." He was made an honorary Canon of Liverpool Cathedral in 1906.

The old cottages near Farnworth Church, one of many old photographs of these cottages. Sadly these thatched cottages are no longer standing, but there are plans to preserve the Bridewell alongside the church.

Ditchfield Hall was not considered to have any architectural features of merit, and so it suffered the fate of so many old buildings in Widnes, being demolished in the early 1960's.

The Chapel inside Ditchfield Hall as found and photographed in 1960, just before the Hall was demolished.

An elderly character who lived in his caravan on Pex Hill. From this picture we can imagine what the long-gone rural area that became Widnes was like before the coming of the chemical industry.

A very different character was the Rev. George Gordon Dawson, pictured here with his wife. Vicar of St. Ambrose from 1919 to 1932, he is described as a notable scholar and seemed to be feared and revered by his congregation in equal measure, yet the church was full during his ministry at St. Ambrose.

Mark Johnson on the tower of his farmhouse in Moorfield Road. Mark was well known in the area and had a local milk round.

Mark Johnson's farmhouse was a distinctive building with its tower and clock face. Though apparently in a reasonable state of repair, it followed many old Widnes buildings and was demolished and the site used for new houses.

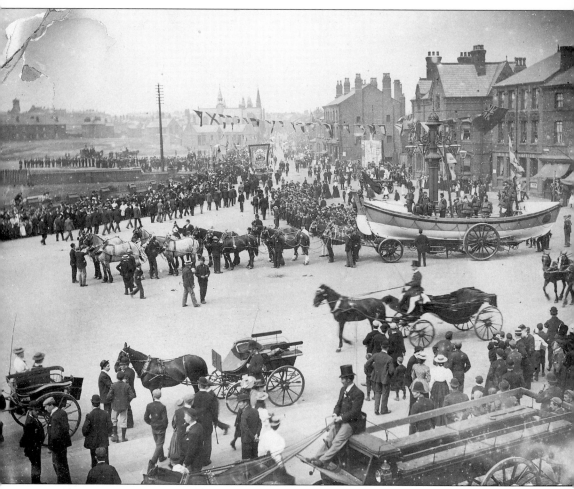

An interesting event was Lifeboat Day in Victoria Square. This was the day when a lifeboat was brought to Widnes for a publicity and money-raising event. On this occasion, before the turn of the century – not a motor vehicle in sight, even the bus in the foreground is horse-drawn – the lifeboat has certainly drawn the crowds, both to watch and take part in the parade. Ten horses are lined-up ready to pull the lifeboat and one wonders how it got to Widnes, was it pulled here by the horses, or did it sail up the river to the Docks? Simm's Cross School can be seen in the middle distance, and on the left we can see clear through to Appleton village and St. Bede's Church. Someone has left their walking-stick on the 'bus'.

The Christie family photographed with their staff in 1896. The family lived at "The Hawthorns" in Derby Road. The house has since been demolished.

The new Horns Hotel at the junction of Moorfield Road and Derby Road. The Horns was demolished recently when the Widnes Eastern by-pass was built on the route of the St. Helens and Runcorn Gap Railway along the "Bongs" – the local name for the valley which the railway shared with Bowers Brook. The Hawthorns mentioned above was in Derby Road which can be seen winding between the cottage on the left and the houses in the centre.

The "Beauties" of Widnes cannot be exaggerated. we are too busy to write.

To close the book we have two examples of the use local photographers made of their pictures of the Widnes area, transforming them into postcards for sale to the locals. In the lower example a pleasant view of West Bank Promenade is used and, above, a young couple are seen relaxing on the river bank near the Transporter Bridge. Perhaps Widnes wasn't that bad a place after all.

THE GREAT SPAN OVER THE MERSEY, 1000 FEET, LINKING, LANCASHIRE TO CHESHIRE, OPENED, 29/5/05.